THE
REMARKABLE

D1666863

TRACY BELL

ISBN 978-1-68570-747-7 (paperback)
ISBN 978-1-68570-748-4 (digital)

Christian Faith Publishing
832 Park Avenue
Meadville, PA 16335
www.christianfaithpublishing.com

Printed in the United States of America

"O house of Israel, can I not do with you as this potter?" says the Lord. "Look, as the clay *is* in the potter's hand, so *are* you in My hand, O house of Israel!"

—Jeremiah 18:6

CONTENTS

Contents

INTRODUCTION

The intention of this book is to encourage and ensure you that you are exactly where you are supposed to be at this time in your life. Whether you are incarcerated in prison or on your way to Vegas for your honeymoon, I believe that the One who created you has placed this book in your path to reveal and remind you who you are, where you are spiritually, and how to navigate toward the purpose and plan that God has for your life.

None of us are supposed to stay where we are forever. Everything is changing within us and around us by the millisecond. Therefore, in order for you and I to transform and move toward our purpose in life, we must change as well. I believe that no puppy dog desires to be a puppy for life any more than a caterpillar desires to stay shut up in its cocoon for eternity. The puppy German Shepherd, Bloodhound, or Poodle instinctively desires to mature, develop, and ultimately fulfill its purpose by pleasing its master. Likewise, the once caterpillar that has transformed into a chrysalis in its cocoon patiently awaits further transformation toward someday becoming a beautiful butterfly, so it may soar into its destiny.

So what about you? Are you aware that you and I also have a master to please and obey? Just as no thoroughbred animal can properly care for itself or train itself to run and win victoriously, it is all the more vital for mankind to acknowledge that apart from its master creator, we cannot run successfully or fulfill our purpose on the earth and please our master-maker and trainer. Is it time for you to take flight into your destiny despite your age, educational status, financial status, skin complexion, or any other handicap that you may claim? I do not think that your destiny will automatically happen just because you were born.

God had plans for Adam and Eve, but they choose to follow the instructions of the master of deception, which eventually cost them an alarming amount that neither could pay $$. As the soon-to-be monarch butterfly instinctively yields to the stages and steps that have been ordered for its life, you and I should likewise be aware that there are stages and steps for our life that have been preordered individually for each of us.

This book is not necessarily intended to make you a billionaire, the governor of your state, the mayor of your town, or the president of your homeowner's association. Its primary purpose is to encourage you to be the ultimate and splendid you that no one else can be but you if you are willing to follow the voice of the master-maker who has given you life. Don't settle for a comfortable C in life. Today is your day to instinctively soar into the high attitudes for your A.

Once your mind is made up to yield to the voice of your master, you will be shaped into a thoroughbred that's fulfilling its purpose. No force will be able to stop you. No weapon, demonic force, pain, alien, disease, addiction, child, spouse, in-laws, career, credit report, or religious people can stop your purpose or your destiny once you decide to yield to the hands of the master-potter, who has called you out of the darkness into His marvelous light.

This transformation will require your faith, obedience, and a power that is much greater than your own. Despite your age and your plans, the One who has kept you so far has greater plans just for you. The master-potter literally has a blueprint of the finished product that He desires you to become. There is a purpose for you and expectations of you.

By the end of this book, hopefully, we will accept and submit to the fact that our will is not going to be the finished product once the potter is done molding us. As we yield to His will, God will lovingly and gently help us to put His agenda and plans ahead of our own.

Paul the apostle said it best in 1 Corinthians 13:11, "When I was a child, I spoke as a child, I understood as a child, I thought as a child; but when I became a man, I put away childish things." Christian or non-Christian, by the end of this book, I pray that you will be enlightened on whose hands you are in and allow those hands to fashion you and shape you into the extraordinary you that the potter is counting on you to be.

CHAPTER 1

GOD MADE YOU

A coincidence is defined as something that happens accidentally without any premeditated plans. When we think of coincidences, we think of things that happen by chance, luck, or fluke right on time or perhaps in the weirdest of times in concert with one another. Before we continue, can we agree on the fact that you are not a coincident or an accident that just so happened to be born to the parents you were born to?

Whether your parents love you dearly or not, I do not believe that they could have ever preplanned in detail the person that you are today and will become tomorrow. You may not personally know both of your biological parents. That's okay because God still used their deoxyribonucleic acid (DNA) to get you on the earth. Some parents may say they would never change one thing about the imperfect us and are grateful that we are the way we are. However, I submit that they could have never predetermined or planned the eyes, hair, nose, heart, mindset, soul, or the spirit that has accommodated our infantile bodies in a trillion light-years. They could have only guessed at best, your gender, height, intellect, and the abilities that you would ultimately possess in life. In spite of the capabilities of ultrasounds in 3D, 4D, and other tests that doctors perform in an effort to determine who you would be and what you would look like, no parent or elite team of doctors could have ever determined who you would become or how you will change the world in small and great ways.

However, according to the Bible, there is Someone who knew you before you were born. According to scripture, there is *Someone* who knows you in such detail that they can tell you the exact numbers of hairs that are on your entire body. There is *Someone* who knows the exact number of breaths that you have taken since you were born. There is *Someone* who knows what makes you happy, sad, fearful, and comfortable. I am confident that there is *Someone* who knows your challenges and your capabilities because that *Someone* was there from the very beginning and knows exactly what you and I are made of.

> You made all the delicate, inner parts of my body and knit them together in my mother's womb. Thank you for making me so wonderfully complex! It is amazing to think about. Your workmanship is marvelous—and how well I know it. You were there while I was being formed in utter seclusion! You saw me before I was born and scheduled each day of my life before I began to breathe. Every day was recorded in your book! (Psalm 139:13–16 Living Bible Translations)

According to Psalm 139, there is only One who is responsible for your initial identity. Before you became you, you had a master designer and architect who had previously drawn up a blueprint of who you were to be from head to toe and from the inside out. Before your mother knew your father, a master builder knew you and made plans concerning you in advance. Before a manufacturer develops a product, the *One* that manufactured you had a design and a purpose that only you could fulfill.

A mother may feel that she accidentally got pregnant, but I submit that the Creator of everything saw the coming together of your two parents and, therefore, beforehand designed a blueprint for your life. Your life was in His hands all the while, and it was the "Creator of the universe" that allowed you to come forward with life from the womb of your mother for a purpose that nobody but you can fulfill.

> The Lord said to me, "I knew you before you were formed within your mother's womb; before you were born I sanctified you and appointed you as my spokesman to the world." (Jeremiah 1:4–5 Living Translation Bible)

In the book of Jeremiah, God was speaking to Jeremiah and reassuring him that He knew him before he was conceived, so plans were made in advance for his life. In time, Jeremiah became a representative, a prophet, and a great man for God. God also foreknew you and me and has set up some appointments for us. Perhaps God did not make appointments for us to be prophets, preachers, teachers, evangelists, pastors, or billionaires; but surely, we have a purpose to do something on the earth that is far greater than our own strength, resources, and capabilities.

Before a builder builds, the first thing he/she needs is a purpose to build. A builder is not likely to build a building, a house, a bridge, a tunnel, and so forth unless there is a purpose for it. A builder will not build a tunnel or a bridge that leads to nowhere. I don't think that a builder would build a skyscraper or a house that he felt he couldn't sell or live in. Therefore, before a builder invests their time, money, and resources, she/he will count up the cost in an effort to be confident that the finished product is worth the investment and is confident that there will be a return on the investment.

Some artists may paint or develop a sculpture just to look at and admire. People may plant flowerbeds with expectations that they will flourish and bring beauty. Likewise, I believe that when mankind was created in the garden, our Creator admired us. I further believe that our Creator planted us in the garden so that we would flourish. Yet there's so much more. As a house is built to be a dwelling place, I believe that God made you and me to be *a dwelling place* for Himself to live in.

You may wonder why God would want to live in someone as imperfect as we are. Well, that's the very reason. As intricate and delicate as God made us, we were all born with imperfections, due to the original sin of our forefathers (Adam and Eve). The Living Bible Translation of Psalm 51:5 says, "But I was born a sinner, yes, from the moment my mother conceived me." It is believed that David, the king of Israel, wrote Psalm 51 after being confronted by a prophet named Nathan, following the king's encounter with Bathsheba, who was the wife of a man named Uriah.

My case and point is this: Though God made us out of the dirt of ground in His image, mankind's image of God has been marred, blemished, and disfigured following some deception that took place in the Garden of Eden by Satan, who continues to be the master of deception. God's plan of action in an effort to get us back to our rightful place in paradise was to reveal to us the height, the depth, and the width of His love. The penalty of what our forefathers did was spiritual separation from God and ultimately physical death.

This would have meant that life for mankind would have ceased, and you wouldn't be reading right now. As a matter of fact, life for everything almost came to an end when it rained for forty days and nights, and water covered the entire earth. However, due to the unsearchable and endless love that God had for mankind, He used the faith of a man named Noah to build an ark, which was a large box-like boat that floated.

By Noah's family entering into the boat on time, their life was spared, and mankind was given another chance. In the process of time, the earth repopulated, and God rebuilt a relationship with man by way of us placing our faith in the fact that He was just who He said He was. Ultimately, whether you consider yourself a Christian or not, you have heard of God's master plan to redeem us, restore us, and get us back on track for our original purpose on the earth. God had to use the life of Someone who was perfect and willing to die on behalf of humanity.

Jesus Christ was the only one who had lived a perfect life and was willing to die on behalf of mankind. Jesus Christ fulfilled the penalty of sin and satisfied the debt that mankind owed with His life.

This one act now enables all who believes and places their faith in this fact the honor and privilege to get back into paradise. You may be a very nice person who pays taxes, goes to church, and treats everybody right. Unfortunately, your civic and righteous acts of kindness will not get you back into paradise. You may serve on the local school's PTA, Girl Scouts, Boy Scouts, or HOA, yet this alone will not get you into a proper relationship with the Creator, where you can begin to fulfill your purpose.

Are you confident that you have accepted Christ in your heart? If your heart is tender enough, you can begin a *new life* today. What do you expect to happen when you flip your light switch on? You probably expect the light to come on, especially if you've paid the light bill. Likewise, when you press the power button to your TV remote control, you expect to see a picture, assuming that you have paid your cable bill. Likewise, when you impart your faith concerning what happened on Calvary, a light will turn on in your soul because you believe that the bill has been paid in full for your power source.

We begin to live for the very first time when we infuse our faith in what Christ did on Calvary. *Today* may be the perfect time for you to be submerged into this liquid and tangible love. Repeat after me this simple prayer:

Lord God, I thank You for sending Your precious and perfect Son, Jesus Christ, into the world for a sinner like me. Jesus, I thank You for publicly dying in my place and giving me this opportunity to make it into heaven when my physical body dies. I put this small measure of faith that I have in You. Please forgive me for all of my sinful ways and thoughts. Lord God, as I accept the price that Jesus paid on Calvary with His life, which was good enough and sufficient for you. I believe that because of Your grace (clemency) and Your mercy (sympathy), I am saved from hell because You just took up residence in my heart and in my life. Thank you, oh, God, for saving me.

Welcome to the body of Christ, my friend. I know it all seems too simple, but that's really all it takes. Neither you nor I could have ever earned our way into heaven without Him (Jesus, *the Son of God*). All we could do was to believe in someone who was good enough to get us in. Jesus just got you in. So now I want you to take a few moments and talk to God in your own words and thank Him for what just took place in your life. It does not matter how you feel. What matters is that you believe in what just took place in your life. I encourage you to stop here and read Psalm 139. Read it for the second time and then talk to God the best way you know how before you continue with chapter 2.

THE PROCESS CONTINUES

The word which came to Jeremiah from the Lord, saying,
Arise, and go down to the potter's house, and there I will cause thee
to hear my words. Then I went down to the potter's house, and,
behold, he wrought a work on the wheels. And the vessel that he
made of clay was marred in the hand of the potter: so he made it
again another vessel, as seemed good to the potter to make it. Then
the word of the Lord came to me, saying, O house of Israel, cannot
I do with you as this potter? saith the Lord. Behold, as the clay is
in the potter's hand, so are ye in mine hand, O house of Israel.

—Jeremiah 18:1–6 (KJV)

When God spoke to Jeremiah concerning the chosen people of Israel, it sounded as if they didn't have a choice or a say so in the plan of God, concerning who they were to become. I remind you that as wonderful as Adam and Eve were made in the beginning, it was their choice to step out of the will and out of the relationship of the One who had formed them in His image. You and I were born and given life by God for a purpose that is far greater than we know. At the end of chapter 1 of this book, I trust that you surrendered your life to God, and you are now born again. This means that since you have applied your faith in what Jesus did for us on Calvary, your soul has been saved, and your whole life is about to change.

You are now in the hands of the potter. The master builder, architect, or potter just began an extreme makeover in your life, beginning with your heart and mind. As wonderful and complex as we are, our life still has some flaws, issues, and character disorders that need to be remodeled and reconditioned. Now that you have a personal, intimate, and meaningful relationship with the potter, the shaping process begins. Shaping into what you say? His image, but it won't happen overnight.

When we are first born, we are not totally complete. When and if you graduated from high school or college, that was just another floor being added to the structure of whom you were becoming. Perhaps you have been married, remarried, retired, and just trying to enjoy life the best you can. All of these chapters of your life were levels and layers of you being built into the ultimate you. Many of the chapters, layers, and chat rooms of our life were good ones. Nevertheless, God permitted us to furnish and plan our life as we saw fit, only so that he could eventually use it for a teaching moment. Experience is still the best teacher. He is now ready to remodel us.

In Jeremiah 18, God was reminding the prophet Jeremiah that as unattractive as His chosen people Israel had become, he was molding, reshaping, and attempting to fashion them into a people that reverenced and respected him. Though Israel was in the hands of God, they would often attempt to leave the house of the potter and go their own way. Your development, progress, and growth will be established by the act of you remaining on the wheel. The hands of God will always be upon the life of the believer, but it's difficult for the potter to properly shape us when we repeatedly jump off the wheel of the potter in order to do our own will.

Remember, we are not battery-operated robots or puppets on a string. Even the born-again believer often finds a justifiable way to turn to the left, though we specifically read and heard the potter say "go right."

I need to remind you that there never was and never will be another you. You may be what they call an identical twin, but your identical twin is not identically like you. He or she may look like you, talk like you, and walk like you, but there is only one you that will ever exist. In other words, you are one of a kind, which makes you valuable. The potter is not finished with you yet, so stay on the wheel. You are one of a kind. You are exquisite, priceless, precious, prized, and remarkable; but your design is not complete, so stay on the potter's wheel. You may be overweight, but you have a purpose. You may have gone through some bad relationships, but you are still cherished and loved. You may have lost loved ones, but you have not lost your life.

Your life is slowly transforming into something magnificent, so stay on the wheel of the potter. You may have health issues and handicaps, but your life is still indispensable and essential to the master builder and potter. Your self-esteem and energy levels may be low today, but if you will stay in the hands of the potter, very soon your praises will be high, and the joy of the Lord will be your strength. You are a treasure that is more valuable than the paintings of Michelangelo, Leonardo da Vinci, Rembrandt, and Picasso all put together. As a matter of fact, what people saw as discrepancies, flaws, and inconsistencies in your life will turn out to be the things that make your Charlie Brown design so unique.

None of our past life ever caught God by surprise. Everything concerning you is now right on course. God is aware that there will be times when you will want to run away from Him and do your own thing. Though you are being transformed in God's hands, it will be your choice to be committed on a daily basis.

God is aware that there will be times when we will feel that He is not moving fast enough. There will be times when we will feel that the plan and the pain that God is allowing in our lives is too great for us to continue with Him. I don't know what God is attempting to fashion you into. What I do know is that it is a process that will require time and patience. How much time, how much patience, and how much commitment will it take? As long as it takes and as much as it takes. God may be attempting to design you to be a tailored suit, by Jones of New York. Please don't decide to jump out of the hands of the potter seamstress and settle to be a rag. Maybe God is in the process of transforming you into a Maserati or a '57 Chevy that's in mint condition. Don't decide to be a grocery cart with three wheels, and two of them are bad.

Most of us can come up with 101 reasons to stay in our comfort zone where we feel safe. As a matter of fact, let me help you: (1) I just don't have the time. (2) I just don't have the strength or the health. (3) I'm too old now. (4) There are some things in my life that I just don't want to let go of right now. (5) I just don't have any support. (6) I'm just trying to do the best that I can.

May I give you just two good reasons why you should surrender to the hands of the potter and master builder? (1) He sees and knows the value of what He has placed inside of you. There are many arrogant people in the world and the church. All of the haughty and egotistic people will be humbled someday. But for those who undervalue your worth, never forget that no man could have ever made you.

You should take a moment and touch yourself and say, "I'm one of a kind, and I'm valuable." Let's try that again, only this time place your hand over your heart and say it confidently. "I AM VALUABLE!" The rarer or fewer you are, the more expensive you become. The mold that you came from has been broken. People may overlook you every day, never realizing that they could have just met a great Charlie Brown, Lucy, or whoever the fabulous you that you are. Are you understanding me now? No amount of gold, rubies, or diamonds can be compared to you.

I know you may not feel like much at times, but take a moment and read what God thinks about you in Psalm 8. Following that, read the first chapter of the Gospel of John verses 1–14 and discover who else had a hand in on you becoming you. Following that reading, relax, mediate, and celebrate the new you before continuing to chapter 3.

CHAPTER 3

OPPOSITION BUILDS CHARACTER

I am a 1980 high school graduate of Garner Senior High School which is located minutes from Raleigh, North Carolina. I considered myself an athlete and believed that I excelled somewhat in track and football in my high school days. I was honored to play for the Garner Trojan varsity football team for three years. I was cocaptain of the football team my senior year, and due to a great frontline blocking, I manage to rush for over one thousand yards that year. I went on to be voted as an all-conference running back that year as well. I received a couple of rewards in track and field also.

I am attempting to paint you a picture of how these high school achievements came to be. I'm sure I don't have to tell you that there was a price to pay for every award that I achieved. Some may have felt that I was just a gifted runner. I may have had the gift, but the gift had to be perfected. Attempting to perfect that teenage gift cost me time and rigorous practices for years. I actually began playing football officially at the age of nine in the Pop Warner league. But in high school, we practiced Monday through Thursday, and game day was on Friday. Football wasn't just for fun anymore because some of us were depending on this game to get us to the next level for educational and eventually economical purposes.

Did you know that some people go to church just for fun and to be entertained or to entertain? There is a place and a time for entertainment, but the primary purpose for your life in the church is to be trained, equipped, and sent out into the world to be light. In high school football, everything that had been rehearsed and practiced over and over again during the week had to be tried by the opposing team on Friday night. There were no exceptions or excuses for not giving 110 percent at practice or during the game.

Our coaches would yell, cuss, and fuss daily because they saw something in us that they were determined to get out of us. They would run us, run over us, hit us upside the head, and, at the end of the day, say something like, "Good job, Tracy Bell! We'll see ya tomorrow." We knew these men were preparing us for our opponents daily, though it often felt like they were the giant Goliaths that we had to endure for hours a day. We had a series of exercises to do daily. We had to run and run and then run some more. We had resistant training with weights, which built our muscles. We had obstacles that we had to run through that sharpened our agility and increased our mobility to move swiftly and maintain balance simultaneously. Many other exercises were designed to build endurance, character, and confidence to overcome any opponent who dared to step on the field with us. Personally, I was so determined to be at the top of my game that I would often go home after practice and work out again.

In one newspaper quote, I can recall my head coach (Bud Deters) say though I was small at 170 pounds, I was the strongest on the team. Many didn't know that I would go home and work out more. Pushups, weight lifting, running, and more. I did this because I was smaller than most. Yet I understood the science of going the extra mile in order to get the most out of what I had to work with. Though it was uncomfortable for me, I felt that if I went home and worked out while my opponents from other high schools went home and reclined, then I might have the upper hand, be more productive, and come out victorious on game day.

At the very least, I expected that I would be able to be prepared for a fair fight. Though the training exercises my coaches provided were in opposition to my mind, my muscles, and my time, it was also what shaped me into a productive sportsman. A true sportsman is not necessarily one who scores all of the points or is named the most valuable player. A true sportsman is one who plays the game with character on the field and off the field and gives his or her best. My Christian definition of character is an individual maintains integrity on Sunday morning at church, Friday night, or payday when he or she is out of town. Ouch! My case and point is this: It was the pain of my opposition that shaped my character and brought out the best character and performance.

So my academics were another story. Academically, I often did just enough to get by. My study habits were less than average most of the time. I wasn't slow or illiterate but lazy with the books and would rather choose a girl or a party over an *A* in algebra. I thought that my talent as a running back was more than enough to get me to the next level in college. They need me! NOT so! Do you know there are people in the church who feel like you can't have a good church service without them? I bet you know a couple of people who feel like nobody can do it like they do it. That's my song, and no one can sing "Amazing Grace" like me. Nobody can pray like me or know the best way to utilize the church's finances like I do.

I believe that God seeks character above talent any day. So you are an accountant with your own firm, but does that necessarily qualify you as a good steward or trustee? You can really sing, but is the character, integrity, and life of God manifested through you? Wow! Pastor, if you ain't preaching today, I'm gonna slip away to my home church. Would it be all right with you if the pastor did not recognize you Sunday morning for being the citizen of the month?

God desires to impart His very own character and image into our hearts and minds. This will take intentional sacrifices to get in His presence routinely if you are going to be faithful and productive on game day. By the way, game day is every day that you wake up. Not on Sundays only. Therefore, I must intentionally press my way into His presence in order to get the character, love, and power that it will take for me to defeat the enemy daily.

Has your life been a series of obstacles and opponents that you never saw coming? Did you assume that somehow, someway things would work out, or did you discover your faith needed to have an ingredient called *work* to be mixed in the bowl? Most Christians say that you only need to pray more, fast more, read more, and study more in order to be successful in life. You've tried that, but tragedies, disappoints, mishaps, and difficulties still came your way.

Do the giant obstacles and opponents that come into your life cause you to kind of stay in your comfortable *C* corner, just enough to get by? I wonder how many millions do just enough to get by with a *C* in the algebra of life, if I may say. I don't mean a *C* for character but a *C* for complacency. So your opposition may have been a series of doctor visits for cancer treatment for yourself or a loved one. Your obstacle may be how to manage your bills and your money. I know, there's never enough, right? You may feel that your child or spouse has been your biggest obstacle or opposition. Some of us feel that neighbors, in-laws, coworkers, church members, the government, or an ex-spouse is the culprit of our opposition that's killing our joy. Let me remind you what Joseph said to his brothers many years after they had sold him to strangers.

> But as for you, you meant evil against me; *but* God meant it for good, in order to bring it about as *it is* this day, to save many people alive. Now therefore, do not be afraid; I will provide for you and your little ones. And he comforted them and spoke kindly to them. (Genesis 50:20–21)

Well, I got some great news just for you. Our Creator and God has allowed every obstacle, opponent, and opposing factor to come your way to build us up and not tear us down. They may not mean it for our good, but God does. Dear friend, it is the horrific, distasteful, unwelcomed, uncomfortable, and miserable trials of life that God uses to build our faith muscles and shape our character into the character of His Son, Jesus Christ.

King David learned to pray on his face and on the run due to the opposition and obstacles of his life. Abraham, Isaac, Jacob, Job, Hannah, Ruth, Mary, and many others all prayed because of opponents and the oppositions that life often presents. If you study these great men and women, you will discover that their most sincere prayers went out when they found themselves up against a wall with no personal strength to climb, faith to fight, or patience to wait.

Personally, my most sincere prayers were offered when the pain was too great, the day was so dark, and I felt that I had nowhere else to turn. With hindsight, I probably could have at least turned to others for prayer, but you and I know that our pride is the other enemy that we have to deal with. We will talk more about PRIDE in a future chapter. Apostle Paul also learned to pray when his days became insurmountable.

> So to keep me from becoming conceited because of the surpassing greatness of the revelations, a thorn was given me in the flesh, a messenger of Satan to harass me, to keep me from becoming conceited. Three times I pleaded with the Lord about this, that it should leave me. But he said to me, "My grace is sufficient for you, for my power is made perfect in weakness." Therefore I will boast all the more gladly of my weaknesses, so that the power of Christ may rest upon me. For the sake of Christ, then, I am content with weaknesses, insults, hardships, persecutions, and calamities. For when I am weak, then I am strong. (2 Corinthians 12: 7–10 English Standard Version)

While we're on this subject of our opponents, obstacles, and opposition, let me tell you who the real enemy is. You don't have to believe me, but there is a God who loves you, and there is Satan, who hates you. God allows the enemy to come into the life of His people to build us up. Our faith must be tried and tested. Satan is an opponent that has already been defeated, but he does not want us to know that. Satan is also an obstacle course that we have to run through and not dread to do so all the time.

The Gospel tells us that after Jesus was baptized, He was led into the wilderness by the Holy Spirit of God to be tempted. Jesus was all alone in a place of wilderness for forty days and nights and had to put up with the devil continuously. However, Jesus went through this obstacle and chapter of His life and dealt with His opponent (Satan) with the Word of God. Jesus applied the Word of God. During that forty-day period, it was pretty much one-on-one—Satan and Jesus Christ. Satan could not fool, trick, or deceive Jesus. Unfortunately, Satan fools, tricks, and deceives us daily. We fuss, fight, and blame the spouse, child, neighbor, coworker, in-law, government, or a particular sect of people. THIS JUST IN, MY FRIEND! The real enemy behind the scenes is Satan. Therefore, I must get to know the Word so that I will be able to properly fight a good fight.

Remembering and being able to quote the Word is a good thing. Believing and applying the Word of God is another dimension. When we whole heartily apply by faith what the Bible says, it means that we trust God more than what we feel, what we see, and what people say. When we apply the Word, we place our lives in God's hands. Satan's greatest trick, being the master of deception, is to make us think that he doesn't exist. If there's no devil, then there must not be a hell for any of us to be concerned about.

"You only live once, so live while you can," is Satan's demonology, but we are wiser than that. The real opposition and enemy is not one who is wrapped in flesh and blood. The real enemy is not the republicans, democrats, independents, or tea parties. It is Satan and his spiritual wickedness in high places. The real enemy is not the police, gangs, or Isis, but Satan. Satan has the okay to use any of the nicest people that you will ever want to meet that are not a part of the body of Christ. They may go to church and do Bible study, but that does not necessarily mean that they are part of the body. Satan can also use any Christian who is not wise enough or discerning enough to detect him. Satan may use any prideful pastor or minister, deacon, musician, or church mother that is not discerning of his schemes because of their lack of character and ongoing intimacy with the Holy Spirit of God.

> For our struggle is not against *flesh and blood*, but against the rulers, against the authorities, against the powers of this dark world and

against the spiritual forces of evil in the heavenly realms. (Ephesians 6:12)

Satan is the head of the dark world who desires to keep us in the dark. He does not want us to know that he exists, so he disguises himself and works through the minds and hearts of people in an effort to keep us feeling fearful, mad, depressed, hopeless, and unproductive on game day, which is every day. Jesus Christ came in order that we may have life, joy, peace, and hope. Some of us may feel that we have a great life, great job, great marriage, and so forth. This could lead to arrogance, a false sense of security, pride, and ultimately causing us to do whatever we got to do to make ourselves happy.

Let me prove my point. Suppose you made a million dollars a year for doing absolutely nothing but traveling the globe anywhere you wanted and anytime you wanted to go. On top of that, your dream spouse gave you all of your heart's desires, and you had the perfect kids, who excelled in everything. However, you get a call from the doctor who says that you need to come into the office ASAP! Long story short, you have an incurable disease (ALS, stage four cancer, or Alzheimer's). Still happy?

By the end of this book, I pray you will be happy that you read it and discover true joy.

CHAPTER 4

NO PAIN, NO GAIN

"No pain, no gain," was one of my football coaches' favorite sayings. I'm sure that many of you have heard this old cliché if you've played any sports for any length of time. What the coaches were trying to tell us was that there was a price to pay in building and strengthening our muscles, mindset, and techniques for game day.

I told you all the rhetoric about my little glory days of track and football for a reason. My coaches used obstacles, weight training tools, and even some choice of words that opposed my muscles and my mind all in an effort to build me up. Likewise, I believe that God uses obstacles in life, such as pain from people, fear of financial debts, addictions, and sickness at times to gently lead us further into His corner for direction, comfort, prayer, repair, revival, and ultimately into His will for our lives.

I do not believe that God intends for us to become totally dull to pain or to develop a skin so thick that the pain or the fear goes away. However, I do believe that we can find a calmness in the midst of our storms simply by developing an awareness of His presence and actually feeling Him in the storm with us. In short, I say that it is God's desire for us to be humbly broken by pain or fear to the point that it would cause us to run into His arms and stay there for a lifetime.

Often, we run to God when we find ourselves in trouble, in pain, in debt, or in fear. We usually stay with Him until we can see the sun shining again on our parade. After that, we gradually go back to doing our thing our way because we can see that the sky is blue again. I can remember partying and sometimes becoming sick and broke. Of course, I would say or at least think those famous words, "Oh, God, help me!" A few days later, the hangover is gone, I got no one pregnant, and the liquor store is open. IT'S ON! Seriously speaking, God desires us to run to Him for a lifetime and not just only in times of trouble. David the King said it best in Psalm 51:16–17.

> For you will not delight in sacrifice, or I would give it; you will not be pleased with a burnt offering. The sacrifices of God are a *broken spirit;* a broken and contrite heart, O God, you will not despise. (Psalm 51:16–17)

I interpret this as God seeking a spirit, soul, and mind that is sincerely humbled and broken for a lifetime with Him. King David says that God does not delight or find pleasure or amusement in our charities, fasts, or prayers unless it leads us to be broken for Him. In other words, we can feed the homeless, clothe the naked, and visit the sick and shut-in. Many of us like to feed the homeless at the shelters around Thanksgiving and Christmas. Many of us do cancer walks and go to funerals to comfort the bereaved families, and all of this is "GREAT!" Not only is it great, but it also gives us a feeling that we have accomplished something. However, do I make the sacrifices that I do because I think it's just the right thing to do, or am I intimate enough with God that I hear Him and follow His voice?

Please be mindful that you and I are representatives of a GREATER kingdom than the physical one we live in. There are two kingdoms, by the way. We represent one of the two daily. Homeless people need to eat every day the last time I checked. Peoples' pain who lose their loved ones lasts beyond the committal in the cemetery and the dining repass. People who are dealing with critical diseases need attention and prayers beyond checking out of the hospital. So I ask myself this question, "Do I do what I do because I hear the voice of God, or do I just need to feel good about myself?"

If my church is not doing a particular thing, does that mean that I don't need to be involved with it? Does everything need to come through the pastor? I thank God for my pastor and Christ-centered pastors throughout the land, but shouldn't God have a direct line with us individually? Is God able to speak directly to you at times without an interpreter? If not, why not? If we are honest, are there some things that we do for our very own glory and recognition? If so, then I'm afraid that our works may be in vain, useless, and perhaps ineffective for the kingdom. I am not saying that you need to feed at the soup kitchen every day, visit the sick weekly, or call all of the new disciples once a week. But I do recommend that you begin to understand that if we are going to follow Him (Jesus Christ), the ride is not going to always be easy if we are going to be effective.

You may be a Christian who just wants to make it into the kingdom, and that's a good thing. However, I must remind you that when Jesus first called His disciples, He said, "Follow Me and I will make you fishers of men." This means that God has not called us so that we may simply be with Him someday. But so that we may offer a ride to others, as we journey through this earthly life. Let's go back to the Bible and recall some obstacles and opponents that broke the back of pride but built the character at the end of the day.

Genesis tells us that Abraham's obstacles and opponents included King Abimelech, a nephew named Lot, a wife named Sarah, a son named Ishmael, and the baby's mamma (Hagar). Before his life was over, Abraham had earned a way into the Hall of Faith by being intimate with God in the midst of it all. There are many others who I can name, but I hope you understand by now that every dark trial that has come your way needed to get God's okay first.

Ask Job. Your faith muscles had to be tested if they were going to grow and mature. Therefore, you can rejoice at the fact that God sees something in you that needs to be built up into a beautiful life for His glory. I have a few questions for you. How prideful are you? Would your character be more attractive if you were less prideful and humbler? What would God have to do in your life to cause you to be more concerned about others and less concerned about things going the way that you had planned? If God spoke to you right now, would you hear Him? Let's take a spiritual break for a few minutes as I attempt to let God Himself speak to you straight out of glory from His very own mouth.

In Romans 9:21,

> Does not the potter have power over the clay, from the same lump to make one vessel for honor and another for dishonor?

In John 1:1–3,

> In the beginning there was the Word. The Word was with God, and the Word was God. He was with God in the beginning. *All things were made by him, and nothing was made without him.*

In John 1:14,

> *The Word became a human and lived among us.* We saw his glory—the glory that belongs to the only Son of the Father—and he was full of grace and truth.

In John 15:13–14,

> The greatest love a person can show is to die for his friends. You are my friends if you do what I command you. (NCV)

These verses simply say that Jesus Christ was always here from the very beginning, and He (God the Son) created everything. You'll have to study John chapter 1 for yourself to understand this. According to the scriptures, Jesus eventually took on the nature of a physical human being that we could see, and He eventually died because He considered us His friends. I'll explain in more detail a bit later. But for now, try to digest the fact that someone thought that you were worth dying for. Jesus Christ, who also happened to be God the Son, thought that you were worth dying for. Wow! Can love get any deeper than that?

We will discuss the importance of dying spiritually later, but the death Jesus Christ had was a physical and painful death, which was significant and necessary in order for us to have a bridge that we could cross away from the death sentence that Satan desires for us. Yes! Jesus is the bridge to eternal life that will help us to escape hell.

If you are not 100 percent confident where you will end up after you die, I would like and I think the One who allowed you to be born (God) would love for you to surrender your life into His hands at this very moment. You don't have to wait until Sunday morning. That's a day that you may never see. You may very well go to church and do a lot of *GREAT* things in church and away from the church. However, are you sure that you've done the one thing that really matters, which denies your very own life for the life that He has in store for you? Is it possible that God, the master-builder of your life, has significantly and intentionally placed your family, friends, coworkers, neighbors, associates, the good, the bad, and the ugly and this book that you are reading strategically, because this is your time to say, "I do"?

You may not want to hear this, but there are people who have been placed in your path that you don't like who need your help. There is an unhappy marriage that only you and God know about. There is someone with cancer who has confided in you, and they feel hopeless. Perhaps it is a lonely senior citizen or someone struggling with an addiction, and they have too much pride to ask anyone for help, but you know. You know the case, but you don't know what to do about it, so you just say, "I'll be praying for you," or "I hope everything works out all right."

Well, my friend, regardless of what side of the fence you're on spiritually, I believe that you got some work to do. Your first step is to mimic what Jesus did on Calvary for the sins of the world. He laid His life down. The voice that I hope you are hearing by now is not asking you to physically die, but to simply trust Him with your heart. The rest of those issues you got going on will be worked out later on down the road. But right now, are you able to admit that you need some help to be more than you are? Remember, we should be evolving, becoming, and growing into perfection. I know, you're comfortable right where you are ;-). I'm going to call that comfortable cocoon thinking. But there's more to you that the world needs.

You may have been sent here to encourage a Harriet Tubman, Billy Graham, Mother Teresa, or Martin Luther King Jr. type of person from committing suicide. I have no idea who, what, when, where, or how you will respond when the time comes for you to help someone. What I do know is that my mission in your life is to point you toward your destiny that no one can fulfill like you. Don't stay comfortable in your peaceful cocoon. Take flight and soar into your destiny and encourage someone else to soar with you into the best life ever!

CHAPTER 5

THE FIRST STEP IS THE BIGGEST

I recall a few momentous times in my life over the years, such as graduating from high school, completing overseas tours in the United States Navy, hearing the wife of my life say I do thirty years ago, building my first home, and being installed as a senior pastor of a church, just to name a few.

As my friends and I walked across the stage to receive what I had worked for, I can recall the cheers and the tears of happiness for what had been accomplished in twelve long years. Likewise, when my ship (*USS Seattle*) came into port, after being in the Mediterranean Sea for six months at a time, there were tears and cheers waiting at the pier for us as we returned home from tour. In marriage and ministry, there were equally tears and cheers of happiness for both occasions.

You can probably recall some momentous and significant times in your life as well I bet. Your most memorable moment perhaps didn't take place at the Olympic games. Maybe you didn't score the winning touchdown for your high school in the state champion-ship game. Your most memorable time may be that of a thirty-year retirement from a job or a doctor's report that says, "There's no sign of cancer in your body." There are others who could say that they were looking at a life sentence, but the DNA of another proved their innocence.

So tell me, how would you say that we were able to witness those momentous moments in our life? Most Christians would say that it was by the "grace of God," and I would agree. However, I must add that though God opened the door to victory, it was up to us to walk through the open door. In other words, you and I had a part to play in the mountain we've climbed. Yes, God did provide everything that was needed, yet still, we had to be willing to take the initial step. I was very far from being valedictorian of my class, but I had to press every day, beginning from kindergarten. I sailed through many bodies of water and visited many countries, while serving in the Navy, but initially, I had to sign up. I said "I do" to my wife on February 16, 1991, and she said the same to me, but prior to that, I had to ask her out, spend money, get a good running car, and the list goes on and on. The same is true with ministry. The church didn't just employ me off the streets. I had to initially yield to the voice of God that was calling me to walk with Him and trust Him decades earlier.

My case and point is this: According to Ecclesiastes 7:8, "*The end of a matter is better than the beginning, and the patient in spirit is better than the proud in spirit.*" This statement informs us that the most difficult is often the first step, and one must be patient in order to *finish successfully.*

I took my wife to the prom in 1979, but it was not until 1991 before I got her to the altar to finally say, "I do." I received an honorable discharge from the Navy in 1985, but prior to that, I had to press my way to the recruiter's office, take tests, sign papers, and make it through boot camp. I received high school awards in sports, but my preparation actually began at the age of eight.

Likewise, before you could retire from your job, you likely had to go to interviews and receive some type of training before finally making it to your retirement celebration. Before you got the good news from your doctor, you had to deal with appointments, prescriptions, paperwork, insurance issues, and Lord knows whatever else before you were able to receive a good report. Let me say it like this: Whenever I go to the beach, that very first step into the water is always the coldest. But once I get myself in, I'M GOOD! *Case and point* is, your initial step of becoming the unique you will be the most difficult, but one day, there is going to be a celebration of cheers and tears of joy! I promise you! But you must be willing to get into the water and flow with the master's plan.

Every architect needs land to complete his/her structure. If there is no land to build on, then the architect will only have skillfully designed blueprints of what he/she desires to come into manifestation. Friend, you are the land that God desires to build upon. You are not yet complete! However, God is still willing to mold, shape, design, and make anyone into someone beautiful inside and out. Your blueprint is in God's hands whether you believe it or not. However, God will not force "His will" onto your territory. The first step is to allow the "master architect" to complete what "He began" from the womb of your mother. This will take a lifetime. Some of us may consider ourselves successful based on our income, status, awards, accomplishments, and the like.

However, Proverbs 9:10 says, "The Fear of the Lord is the *beginning of wisdom*." In my opinion, King Solomon is informing us that we don't know anything until we began to respect, acknowledge, and reverence "the One" who initiated our human fetus, which will continue to transform for the rest of our life.

I believe Solomon is qualified to speak on wisdom because he had accomplished so much in various ways. Though Solomon had amassed more revenue, land, houses, and women than most can only dream about, he concluded at the end of the day that it meant nothing, unless there was a relational knowing and awe of your "master builder." Solomon warns us that all the world has to offer is meaningless until we recognize where true life begins. When I say *true life*, I am talking about eternal life, which only comes by way of knowing God our creator personally.

Having wealth and influence can be a good thing, but wealth and influence are futile without an intimate awareness and connection to God, which we gain by placing our faith in His Son, whom He sent as a ransom for our lives. That's just how valuable we are to Him. What family member would you give in an effort to free some stranger from death row? EXACTLY! Nevertheless, God shows us how great His love is for us who are strangers by sending His Son whom He loves dearly.

If I may recap, (1) we will never begin to walk in our true purpose outside of Him. We may achieve our dreams and aspirations, but that's not necessarily our ultimate purpose in life. You may become a millionaire, walk the red carpet, or win Grammys and Super Bowl championships, but our purpose in life supersedes these things, and we will be *unable* to fulfill our ultimate meaningful purpose apart from Him. (2) Though the architect, the builder, and the project manager are all in one, they cannot build on just any land. The foundation must be suitable for the building if the building is going to be erected and established. If a building or house is built on a foundation that is unsuitable, then the structure will not stand. Our Creator, the master builder, cannot build on us until we acknowledge and allow Him to be our foundation.

God desires for us to be rectified and established in His hands and according to His will. Again, He will not force His will or His blueprint onto our property unless we are willing. God is a gentleman. He may allow obstacles and stumbling blocks to come into our life all in an effort to help us yield to His will. God *is not* asking you to drop every sin in your life so that He can start building you into someone beautiful, but He is simply saying, "*Trust Me* and my *Son Jesus* that I sent on your behalf and that will be the beginning of the building project." (3) Finally, it's going to take a minute before the project is completed so be patient with the builder. Your house that is being built, and those that the project manager will send your way to complete you, will finish you right on time. Paul the apostle said it best in Philippians 3:12–14,

> Not that I have already attained or am already perfected; but I press on, that I may lay hold of that for which Christ Jesus has also laid hold of me. Brethren, I do not count myself to have apprehended; but one thing I do, forgetting those things which are behind and reaching forward to those things which are ahead, I press toward the goal for the prize of the upward call of God in Christ Jesus.

This super chief-apostle is transparent enough to inform us that he is not there yet. Though he has learned from the best of schools and has done momentous things for the kingdom of God, we see here that he admits that he is still a work in process. Though the great man has taught the Gospel and preached the Gospel far and near, he is humble enough to enlighten us that he is not perfect, and his mission is incomplete.

Is it necessary for me to say that you will never reach perfection? Though you are as remarkable as you are and extraordinary, you will likely never meet your full potential on planet earth or any other planet. If you could reach your full potential, then you would be exactly like Jesus was while He lived on earth. But because you are presently housed in your fleshly humanity, perfection is not possible.

Nevertheless, Paul continues to press and strive to become like Jesus Christ. The apostle's effort toward perfection is not by keeping biblical laws but by obtaining the mind of Jesus Christ. Paul understands that if he apprehends the mind of Christ. then he may, in time, develop the heart of Christ, which will enable him to live the life of Christ.

Think of it like this; you may safely drive at fifty-five, properly stop at all stoplights, and observe all traffic signs and all the rules and laws while driving. But guess what, that does not necessarily mean that you are a good driver. It means you are a safe driver. There is nothing wrong with a safe driver, but if I'm a patient in an ambulance who just had a heart attack, then I want a good driver who can get me there fast and safe.

If an intruder breaks into my home, and my wife is there alone, I need the policeman or policewomen to get there as fast as possible. The Bible gives us examples where the need of persons superseded laws, rules, and regulations. See Matthew 12:1–14, Matthew 15:1–20, John 8:3–11, and Luke 6:1–11 for more insight. My case and point is this: Once we take the very first leap of faith toward trusting Jesus as Savior, Lord and King, that will only be the beginning of our transformation in becoming like Him. It should not be the beginning of how many rules, laws, and biblical regulations we keep. Many of us feel that we are more like Jesus because we do not do the sins that we use to do. Not to willfully sin is a good thing. However, if you took the time to read the previous scriptures, you will see that some of our hearts are full of sin, hate, envy, and judgment that we are not conscious of.

Apostle Paul lets us know that though he is not there, he presses toward a higher and greater calling. Paul accomplished much as a strict keeper of the Law of Moses. Paul was so religious and such a keeper of the law that he, at one time, would have Christians executed. But once he had an encounter with Jesus, his entire world changed for the better. Though he had a terrible past, this now super apostle says, "One thing I do, forgetting those things which are behind and reaching forward to those things which are ahead."

My friend, you cannot take a step into your future and hold onto your past at the same time. Regardless of how bad or how good you think your past was, the remarkable you is waiting for you to let it go and move on to the greater remarkable and splendid you that's only one step at a time away. There is a prize for you at the finish line. Runners, on your mark, get set, go!

CHAPTER 6

MOUNTAINS AND VALLEYS, RIVERS AND OCEANS

I n previous chapters, we have discussed the process, the opposition, the purpose of our pains, and the importance of taking the
very first step in our development toward maturity. If the incredible,
remarkable, and extraordinary you follow the recommended plan, I
am confident that you will have your mountaintop encounters with
God just like Moses. I doubt if you will hear Him, He will verbally
say, "Take off your shoes. You are on holy ground," like He says to
Moses. I further doubt that you will see a bush, a tree, or anything
on fire besides your heart and love. If you are sincere and committed
to fulfilling His will in your life, I am confident that you will meet
Him in such a manner that you will feel His overwhelming presence
fill and flood your heart as only He can. If you apply a few biblical
and practical principles to your life, the wonderful you will have your
mountaintop experience, meaning you will in time "mount up with
wings like an eagle," feeling that nothing will be impossible for you.
There will be times when you will feel like going into the ministry
twenty-five hours a day, eight days a week, for 375 days of the year.
Let's look at Peter the rock who was one of Jesus's right-hand men.

> Peter answered and said to Him, "Even if
> all are made to stumble because of You, I will
> never be made to stumble." Jesus said to him,
> "Assuredly, I say to you that this night, before

the rooster crows, you will deny Me three times."
Peter said to Him, "Even if I have to die with
You, I will not deny You!" (Matthew 26:33–35)

Peter likely thought that he was full of the life of Jesus Christ.
Time tells us that Peter was not as full as he had assumed. Though
Peter has been in a three-year accelerated course with Jesus up close
and personally on a daily basis, and though Peter has truly had some
mountaintop experiences, God tenderly reveals to Peter that he is still
a work in progress. Peter has personally witnessed with his own two
eyes the opening of eyes that had seen anything before.

Peter personally witnessed Jesus heal a multitude of people
without using medication, operating room gadgets, sutures, or any
anesthesia. Peter has seen Jesus feed a multitude of people without a
pot, a pan, or even a kitchen to cook it. Peter has seen Jesus walk on
water and command the wind and the waves to lay down in humble
submission. As a matter of fact, when the militia came to arrest Jesus,
it was Peter who threw the first blow cutting off the ear of who he
considered the enemy. Peter must have felt like David felt when he
got into the ring with Goliath. But, ah, how fast things can change.

Now Peter sat outside in the courtyard. And
a servant girl came to him, saying, "You also were
with Jesus of Galilee." But he denied it before
them all, saying, "I do not know what you are
saying." And when he had gone out to the gate-
way, another girl saw him and said to those who
were there, "This fellow also was with Jesus of
Nazareth." But again he denied with an oath, "I
do not know the Man!" And a little later those
who stood by came up and said to Peter, "Surely
you also are one of them, for your speech betrays
you." Then he began to [o]curse and [p]swear,
saying, "I do not know the Man!" Immediately a
rooster crowed. And Peter remembered the word
of Jesus who had said to him, "Before the rooster

crows, you will deny Me three times." So he went
out and wept bitterly. (Matthew 26:69–75)

Earlier in Matthew 26, while Peter was having his mountaintop
experience, he informs the one who has turned water into wine and
raised the dead back to life that he personally would never stumble
and was ready to die for Him. It took about twenty-four hours for
Peter to have a change of heart and revert back to cursing and swear-
ing that he has never seen Jesus in his life. In short, Peter went from
having a mountaintop experience to plummeting to the deepest valley all in about 0.1 milliseconds.

My point is this: Though there will be times when you will feel like
you can conquer Russia, there will also be brief times when you will not
want to get out of your bed. As you follow the life of Christ, you will
have exuberant mountaintop experiences that you feel will never end.
But just remember that every mountain is connected to a valley- or a
desert-like place. During these valley experiences that you are more than
likely to have, you'll probably ask God to end them immediately. Equally
remember this, God will be with you regardless of the mountain you're
on or the valley you're in. Jehovah God will be the same God with the
same power and the same love for you no matter where you are or how
you feel as you wait on Him to transcend you toward your destiny.

This mountain and valley chapter is only to remind you to keep
fighting the good fight of faith. You won't likely give up on God,
but you'll truly feel like giving up on ministry, people, and perhaps
even life during your valley experiences. As I said earlier in the book,
these experiences are only to build you and never to kill you. These
experiences must come in an effort to prove to you that God is sov-
ereign, in charge, absolute, perfect, majestic, dominant, prevailing,
all-powerful, all-knowing, and complete.

God desires for us to know that He alone supersedes our income,
intellect, education, achievements, strength, resources, social media
followers, family, friends, political party, or any other thing that we
consider valuable assets in our lives. There is no one or nothing that
could ever come close to fulfilling or bringing the peace and joy that
God is able to supply.

As a matter of fact, I believe that God desires for the incredible you to know Him and be more intimate with Him than we are with our spouse, children, parents, lover, friends, or any other being that we hold dear to our heart, including our loving pets. Furthermore, unless He allows us to walk through the valley of the shadow of death, we may never come to intimately know of His overwhelming love and provisions during our dark barren times of life. As a matter of fact, I believe our "valley of the shadow of death" experiences are only tests to strengthen us and cause us to be more aware of His love. I would suggest that this valley leads us to a table that has been set for us in the VIP section for all to see.

I have a few friends who could tell you about mountaintop and valley-low experiences. One of my favorites is Elijah:

> At the time of sacrifice, the prophet Elijah stepped forward and prayed: "Lord, the God of Abraham, Isaac and Israel, let it be known today that you are God in Israel and that I am your servant and have done all these things at your command. *Answer me, Lord, answer me, so these people will know that you, Lord, are God, and that you are turning their hearts back again." Then the fire of the Lord fell and burned up the sacrifice, the wood, the stones and the soil, and also licked up the water in the trench.* When all the people saw this, they fell prostrate and cried, "The Lord—he is God! The Lord—he is God!" (1 Kings 18:36–39)

Oh, my God! I can only imagine how Elijah felt when God immediately responded to his prayer. First of all, who did he think he was to call on God before such a multitude of people? What if God did not respond? What an embarrassment Elijah would have been to the kingdom of God. I believe that Elijah was only doing what God had led him to do, and He was able to lead him because of their intimate relationship. The only thing that could scratch the surface of this mountaintop experience is how a president may feel after winning an election, or how a quarterback may feel after throwing the winning touchdown in the Super Bowl, leaving no time on the clock. THIS WAS TRULY A MOUNTAIN TOP EXPERIENCE THAT LITERALLY TOOK PLACE ON A MOUNTAIN.

But things changed quickly:

> Elijah was afraid and ran for his life. When he came to Beersheba in Judah, he left his servant there, while he himself went a day's journey into the wilderness. He came to a broom bush, sat down under it and prayed that he might die. "I have had enough, LORD," he said. "Take my life; I am no better than my ancestors." Then he lay down under the bush and fell asleep. (1 Kings 19:3–5)

Who would have ever guessed that after achieving such a victory in a chapter earlier, Elijah would be on the run for his life and become depressed to the point of desiring death over life! How soon we find ourselves feeling defeated based on temporary circumstances. When valley-low trouble creeps into our life, we often treat it as though it's permanent. Even one of the greatest prophets ever—Elijah—handled his valley experience as though it was permanent. But just as every mountain has a valley/desert placed next door, likewise every valley or dry barren place has an oasis or hilltop not too far off as well. If you will refuse to live in the moment and continue to move forward, there is another mountain, oasis, and water that will quench your weary soul. Let's go back to Elijah again.

> There he went into a cave and spent the night. And the word of the Lord came to him: "What are you doing here, Elijah?" He replied, "I have been very zealous for the Lord God Almighty. The Israelites have rejected your covenant, torn down your altars, and put your prophets to death with the sword. I am the only one left, and now they are trying to kill me too." The

Lord said, "Go out and stand on the mountain in the presence of the Lord, for the Lord is about to pass by." Then a great and powerful wind tore the mountains apart and shattered the rocks before the Lord, but the Lord was not in the wind. After the wind there was an earthquake, but the Lord was not in the earthquake. After the earthquake came a fire, but the Lord was not in the fire. And after the fire came a gentle whisper. When Elijah heard it, he pulled his cloak over his face and went out and stood at the mouth of the cave. (1 Kings 19:9–13)

Even in our darkness, God will reach out to us to bring us out into His marvelous light. As a matter of fact, I believe God does His best work in our darkest hours. Though Elijah is feeling some kind of a way, we see here how God so lovingly visits him. Notice that God does not visit him on this particular day with horns, trumpets, tambourines, loud-sounding cymbals, and drums. As a matter of fact, during this one-on-one church service encounter, I don't believe there was a sound system in the house or no one dancing in the isles. It was just Elijah and God.

Though there was a lot of noise shaking going on, God wasn't in any of that. Be sure you're able to distinguish the voice of God from the charismatics of people when you're really in the need to hear from Him. There was finally a small still voice, and Elijah recognized the voice. We are reminded in John 10:27 that the people of God recognize the voice of God. If God spoke to you today and told you to stand, would you recognize His voice and stand or stay in your cave of despair?

I pray you will stand on His Word and on His promises today. He won't let you down. There are many others who had mountain and valley experiences, but they all came out on top. Elijah received and obeyed the words that God spoke, and there came an insurmountable amount of rain on the land that had been dry and barren for so long. There will likely be multiple times when God will not send the rain, the money, the healing, or the help that we need RIGHT NOW! However, He promises to be with us no matter how deep we feel we have sunk with no way out. He is there for those of us who trust Him, and His presence will always surpass any amount of money, comfort, or love that mankind can provide. His grace is sufficient.

In the next chapter, we will take a look at the dangers of desiring to live in the past.

CHAPTER 7

THE DANGEROUS PAST

So Lot went out and said to his sons-in-law, who were to marry his daughters, "Up, get out of this place; for the Lord is about to destroy the city." But he seemed to his sons-in-law to be jesting.

—Genesis 19:14

You may already be familiar with the story of how Abraham interceded or intervened on behalf of his nephew Lot, who was living in a place called Sodom with his family. In chapter 18 of the Book of Genesis, God revealed to Abraham that He was going to destroy Sodom and Gomorrah because of their grave wickedness. With Abraham having a family there, he pleaded with God not to destroy this place because there were *righteous* or good godlike people living in that land that he felt should not be destroyed.

God knew that there were far fewer so-called righteous or godlike people living in Sodom and Gomorrah than Abraham thought. Nevertheless, God bargained with Abraham and said that He would not destroy Sodom and Gomorrah if there were at least ten righteous living in that land. Unfortunately, there were less than ten godlike people found in the metropolis of Sodom and Gomorrah. Nevertheless, because of the grace of God and the meticulous care and love that He has for His people, He provided a warning and safe passage out of the land before He commenced a fiery rain from above. God was about to show up and show out once again as He did in the days of Noah; only this time, His fury was not going to come in the form of water but by fire and brimstone.

Shortly before everything hits the fan, two angel agents are sent to warn Lot (the nephew of Abraham) what is about to take place. As Lot makes preparations to leave Sodom, he urges his sons-in-law to get up and get out of this place because it was about to be destroyed, annihilated, devastated, and burned down to nothing. For some reason, Lot's soon-to-be sons-in-law thought he was joking. This was not a joke, a fire drill, or just another localized forest fire.

God was about to rain down fire and brimstone on Sodom because it was full of sin and abomination, including unnatural lust, pride, oppression of the poor, haughtiness, arrogance, and self-importance. *Who or what could destroy this vast, fortified, established city?* was likely what the sons-in-law thought, causing them not to take the warning seriously.

If God told you that it was time to move out of your present place of comfort, what would your response be? Perhaps today's warning is not to move from a geographical location, but from a spiritual location or mindset that you may be comfortably living in. If you were told to move from a place of lust, arrogance, anger, pride, self-centeredness, unforgiveness, jealousy, procrastination, lying, malice, and the like, would you move, or would you think God was joking?

We never heard anything more of the men that were to be married to the daughters of Lot because they thought God was joking. God was not telling jokes on this day but was about to heat up this land just as soon as He got a few of His righteous people out of harm's way.

> When morning dawned, the angels urged Lot, saying, "Get up, take your wife and your two daughters who are here, or else you will be consumed in the punishment of the city." But he lingered; (Genesis 19:15–16)

Though Lot just gave an urgent warning for sons-in-law to be to run for their lives, he lingers. Lot has clearly been warned and instructed to flee from a place called home so that he may avoid the destruction at hand, but he lingers. He believes that imminent danger is at hand, yet he lingers, delays, and procrastinates. He obviously believes because he just ministered this same word to others. I cannot tell you why Lot is lingering, hesitating, delaying, or waiting in a territory that he has been warned to move from. All we know is that if the warning is true, Lot's life will quickly end in a few more verses.

Unfortunately, we all linger, hesitate, and delay longer than we should. I believe that God is loving, kind, and so much more. But I also believe that God keeps His Word. If He said it's going to happen, then it's only just a matter of time before it happens. I believe that some good Christian people get stuck in physical and or spiritual locations when we do not move in the proper time when informed. Most of us linger, procrastinate, and delay often because we don't understand the urgency of the voice of God. We may not instantly die, but we definitely won't succeed in the things of God. Let's see what God does next in the life of Lot and his family.

> And while he lingered, the men took hold of his hand, his wife's hand, and the hands of his two daughters, the Lord being merciful to him, and they brought him out and set him outside the city. So it came to pass, when they had brought them outside, that he said, "Escape for your life! Do not look behind you nor stay anywhere in the plain. Escape to the mountains, lest you be destroyed." (Genesis 19:16–17)

Oh, my! Let's just pause here for a moment and observe the mercies of God. I believe that due to God's covenant with Abraham and Abraham's intercession on behalf of his nephew Lot, the grace and mercy of God pulled Lot and his family out of harm's way. Though they are now out of harm's way, another command is given to keep moving and to don't look back. I equate that as God saying, "Now that I have delivered you, keep it moving!" I believe I hear God say,

"Now that I've gotten you out of the way of trouble, don't continue to look back and play games with trouble any longer."

Can you imagine God delivering us from the bedroom of a troubled love affair into His bedroom so He can get to know us intimately for Himself? If He is a jealous God as the Bible says, then He may have a problem with us desiring something or someone more than we desire Him.

Lot and his family have been physically saved and delivered, but they are not totally out of harm's way. I believe that because of the intense heat of the fire and brimstone that are about to fall, they may still be affected if proper distancing does not take place. Not only are they to keep it moving, but they are not to look back. No turning back, no turning back. As a matter of fact, God would have them to not even desire to live in that past any longer. Don't lust for that or desire that! Run to the hills from that, or you may be consumed. Run to the hills, or the world may consume you. Run to the hills, or the ways of the world may overwhelm you. Run to the hills, or Satan may sift us like wheat, but, "I have prayed for you," says Jesus!

> And Lot said to them, "Oh, no, my lords; your servant has found favor with you, and you have shown me great kindness in saving my life; but I cannot flee to the hills, for fear the disaster will overtake me and I die. Look, that city is near enough to flee to, and it is a little one. Let me escape there—is it not a little one?—and my life will be saved!" He said to him, "Very well, I grant you this favor too, and will not overthrow the city of which you have spoken. Hurry, escape there, for I can do nothing until you arrive there." Therefore the city was called Zoar. The sun had risen on the earth when Lot came to Zoar. (Genesis 19:18–23)

Here we see the mercies of God again as Lot displays that he just can't go any further. "I just can't do anymore," says Lot. Therefore, now that he recognizes that he is dealing with a merciful God who is kind as well, he begs the angels to allow him to make a little nearby town his new dwelling place. Permission is granted, and he is urged to get there, for God will not do what He's going to do until you are out of harm's way.

Wow! I wonder if God is going to do something in a particular place that you're in once He gets you out of harm's way. If God reached down to grab your hand so that He could move you from your place of comfort into His place of safety, would you mutually take Him by the hand or snatch back because you're not ready to leave yet? As a matter of fact, I have heard it said that one day, God is going to save the last soul before He begins to unleash Satan to cause havoc on the earth. I believe that the body of Christ will be raptured up by this time. Yet still, there will be a time when no more warnings will come, and the end will be at hand.

> Then the Lord rained on Sodom and Gomorrah sulfur and fire from the Lord out of heaven; and he overthrew those cities, and all the Plain, and all the inhabitants of the cities, and what grew on the ground. But Lot's wife, behind him, looked back, and she became a pillar of salt. (Genesis 19:14–26)

My dear friend, some people believe that religion, the Bible, and a place called heaven were all made up in an effort to give people a false sense of hope of a secure future. Many believe that hell is just as fake as heaven is, and once you die, you are just dead, and there is nothing left of you that can be salvaged. But what if there is a heaven and a hell? But what if there is Jesus at the end of the day that will give you a thumbs-up or a thumbs-down? Then what?

If you own a house, a car, or some means of transportation, you probably have it all insured in the event that it is damaged or causes damage to the property of another. You likely also have health insurance or a life insurance policy just in case you have an illness that could cost an astronomical amount of money without a policy.

Likewise, most of us have a life insurance policy so that no one will have to pay thousands of dollars to bury us when our time comes.

We insure things, not simply because it is the law, but because we value them, and we dare not want to pay the cost should these things be damaged. So, if they are damaged, we're covered when we have insurance. We are not counting on our properties being damaged, but just in case they are, our insurance covers us.

My case and point is this: I'm pretty confident that one day you and I are going to die. Can we agree on that? Good! My next point is this: Whether we believe in Jesus or don't believe in Jesus, these physical bodies that we presently live will one day become corrupted, degraded, contaminated, and will eventually rot. Can we agree to that? Good! Finally, what if there is a Jesus standing there at the end of time with a book in His hands that contains the names of those who wholeheartedly trusted Him as their personal Lord and Savior? And what if there is a hell that Satan and all others who *did not believe* will be condemned to *for eternity* with unending pain day and night?

In closing, I am confident that this is exactly how it will be. I have the assurance that I am covered when my earthly life is over because my assurance policy was paid up in full when Jesus Christ died on the cross for my sins. I have no fear of death because I am convinced that my physical death is my route to heaven.

On the other hand, what if you or those who never truly believe fail to put their trust in Jesus? Well, if that's the case, I still lost nothing if I end up as dust or come back as a tree or a bird. But if the Bible is true, and I'm convinced that it is, then those who failed to get their assurance have lost everything! Why not get your soul-life insured today? You probably plan to once you get some things behind you, like certain sins, a certain relationship, or a particular bad habit. Well, let me be the first to inform you that none of us can clean ourselves up good enough to be found worthy of the gift of salvation. That's why salvation is free for whosoever. We must come just the way we are regardless of our sinful lifestyles.

People will make you feel like you can't truly be saved if you're living a particular way. I say that if you sinned before you were saved, you will likely sin once you are saved as well. However, the more intimate and acquainted you become with Jesus, the more you will become like Jesus one day at a time.

I pray that this book will inspire you to become the miraculous you that God desires you to be. May God bless you extravagantly, and I'll look forward to seeing you in heaven.

Tracy J. Bell was born in Raleigh, North Carolina, and returned to reside in the area after his enlistment in the United States Navy. Though Tracy was raised in a Christian home by his single-parent mother with four other siblings, he found a way to weave in with whatever everyone else was doing. Nevertheless, in due season, the values that were instilled in Tracy by his caring mother eventually took root, causing Tracy to have an unquenchable love for people regardless of their nationality, social status, political preference, gender, religion, and the like. Tracy's mission and determination to see people reach their full potential and purpose in life have chartered him from the alleys of the homeless to the shelters of Hurricane Katrina and even to the devasted rocky roads of Haiti. On each journey, Tracy saw the same thing: people with value, a purpose, and a destiny to fulfill.

Pastor Tracy was installed as the senior pastor of New Bethel Christian Church in Raleigh, North Carolina, in 2013 along with his amazing wife (Mary) and their four wonderful children. Many in the community refer to Pastor Tracy as "the Community Pastor" because of his vigor and relentless efforts to reach the youth and the loss and bridge the gaps that divide churches from one another and the body of Christ from the community. Pastor Tracy continues to work closely with his pastor (Charles W. Brooks) and his home church family Poplar Springs Christian Church, who gave him a wealth of wisdom, respect, and support during his tenure there.

CPSIA information can be obtained
at www.ICGtesting.com
Printed in the USA
BVHW041418140223
658283BV00041B/672

9 781685 707477